MIX
Papier aus verantwortungsvollen Quellen
Paper from responsible sources
FSC® C105338

Joachim Ntunda

Investigating the challenges of promoting dark tourism in Rwanda

Anchor Compact

Ntunda, Joachim: Investigating the challenges of promoting dark tourism in Rwanda., Hamburg, Anchor Academic Publishing 2014
Original title of the thesis: Investigating the challenges of promoting dark tourism in Rwanda

Buch-ISBN: 978-3-95489-233-4
PDF-eBook-ISBN: 978-3-95489-733-9
Druck/Herstellung: Anchor Academic Publishing, Hamburg, 2014

Bibliografische Information der Deutschen Nationalbibliothek:
Die Deutsche Nationalbibliothek verzeichnet diese Publikation in der Deutschen Nationalbibliografie; detaillierte bibliografische Daten sind im Internet über http://dnb.d-nb.de abrufbar

Bibliographical Information of the German National Library:
The German National Library lists this publication in the German National Bibliography. Detailed bibliographic data can be found at: http://dnb.d-nb.de

All rights reserved. This publication may not be reproduced, stored in a retrieval system or transmitted, in any form or by any means, electronic, mechanical, photocopying, recording or otherwise, without the prior permission of the publishers.

Das Werk einschließlich aller seiner Teile ist urheberrechtlich geschützt. Jede Verwertung außerhalb der Grenzen des Urheberrechtsgesetzes ist ohne Zustimmung des Verlages unzulässig und strafbar. Dies gilt insbesondere für Vervielfältigungen, Übersetzungen, Mikroverfilmungen und die Einspeicherung und Bearbeitung in elektronischen Systemen.

Die Wiedergabe von Gebrauchsnamen, Handelsnamen, Warenbezeichnungen usw. in diesem Werk berechtigt auch ohne besondere Kennzeichnung nicht zu der Annahme, dass solche Namen im Sinne der Warenzeichen- und Markenschutz-Gesetzgebung als frei zu betrachten wären und daher von jedermann benutzt werden dürften.

Die Informationen in diesem Werk wurden mit Sorgfalt erarbeitet. Dennoch können Fehler nicht vollständig ausgeschlossen werden und die Diplomica Verlag GmbH, die Autoren oder Übersetzer übernehmen keine juristische Verantwortung oder irgendeine Haftung für evtl. verbliebene fehlerhafte Angaben und deren Folgen.

Alle Rechte vorbehalten

© Anchor Academic Publishing, ein Imprint der Diplomica® Verlag GmbH
http://www.diplom.de, Hamburg 2014
Printed in Germany

DEDICATION

To my parents my late father Mr, Tharcisee and Peruth
To my family members
To all my friends

ACKNOWLEDGEMENT

An academic research is never possible without the tacit and dedicated support of the supervisor and academic colleagues that verily keep you going and reinforce your intellectual acumen and skills through debate and comparison in terms of academic scores.

My deepest appreciation and thanks go to my supervisor, Mr. Emanuel NSABIMANA for his guidance and constructive criticisms that helped me stay focused from the beginning of this work to the end.

I am highly indebted to Fonds d'Assistance pour les Rescapés du Génocide (FARG) and my family members and relatives for unwavering support and also for material and financial support throughout my education and research work. Thank you for supporting me.

I furthermore, I thank the administration of Rwanda Tourism Univesity college (RTUC) to have confirmed that permission and encouraged me to go ahead with my dissertation.

I would like also to express my heartfelt gratitude to my family members Aunt Mutumwinka Margarite and his husaband Mr. Kayisire calixte my cousin kayisire Solange, my friend Uwabo Josyne, Ntezimana Faustin, Rukundo Emmanuel, Rukundo Benjamin, to my special family

I also want to thank the respondents I used in this study for their help and contribution towards the success of this project.

I also want to thank the respondents I used in this study for their help and contribution towards the success of this project.

I am greatly appreciating my colleagues of the Department of travel and tourism management at Rwanda tourism University College with whom I shared on different subjects for supported cooperation.

TABLE OF CONTENTS

DEDICATION V
ACKNOWLEDGEMENT VI
LIST OF ABBREVIATIONS, ACRONYMS IX
LIST OF TABLES X
LIST OF FIGURES XI
ABSTRACT.. XII
CHAPTER ONE 1
INTRODUCTION AND BACKGROUND TO THE STUDY 1
1.1 Introduction... 1
1.2 Background to the study 1
1.3 Statement of the Problem.. 3
1.4 Purpose of the study.. 4
1.4.1 Objectives of the study... 4
1.4.2 Research questions... 4
1.5 Scope of the study... 4
1.6 Significance of the study... 4
1.7 Structure of the dissertation 5
CHAPTER TWO 6
LITERATURE REVIEW 6
2.0 Introduction... 6
2.1 Definition and explanation of key terms... 6
2.1.1 Tourism... 6
2.1.2 Dark Tourism 7
2.2 Theoretical Overview of Dark Tourism.. 7
2.3 Dark Tourism Products 10
2.3.1 Dark Fun Factories... 10
2.3.2 Dark Exhibitions 10
2.3.3 Dark Dungeons 11
2.3.4 Dark Resting Places 12
2.3.5 Dark Shrines... 12

2.3.6 Dark Conflict Sites 13

2.3.7 Dark Camps of Genocide 14

2.4 The Motivations of Dark Tourism 14

2.4.1 Strategies used in promoting/marketing dark tourism 16

2.4.2 Challenges in marketing/ promoting dark tourism 17

2.5.1 Dark Tourism in Rwanda 19

2.6 Chapter Two Summary 20

CHAPTER THREE 22

RESEARCH METHODOLOGY 22

3.1 Research Design 22

3.3 Study population 22

3.4 Sample size 22

3.5 Sampling procedure 23

3.6 Data Collection Instruments 23

3.8 Data Management and Analysis 24

3.8.1 Qualitative analysis 24

CHAPTER FOUR 26

DATA ANALYSIS AND PRESENATATION 26

4.0 Introduction 26

4.1 Background information of respondents 26

CHAPTER FIVE 38

SUMMARY OF FINDINGS, CONCLUSION AND RECOMMENDATIONS 38

5.1 Summary of Findings 38

5.2 Conclusions 39

5.3 Recommendations 40

REFERENCES 42

APENDIX A: Letter addressing the intention of the research to respondents 46

APENDIX B : Questionnaire 47

QUESTIONNAIRE 47

LIST OF ABBREVIATIONS, ACRONYMS

ASCE: Association of Significant Cemeteries in Europe

FARG: Fonds d'Assistance pour les Rescapés du Génocide / National Assistance Funds for Needy Survivors of Genocide

Mr. Mister

NCRM: National Civil Rights Museum

RDB: Rwanda Development Board

Reg No: Registration number

RTUC: Rwanda Tourism University College

U.K: United Kingdom

UAS: United Arab States

US: United States

WTO: World Tourism Organization

LIST OF TABLES

Table 1: Dark tourism products and place 29
Table 2: Less effective information dissemination 30
Table 3: High cost charged to tourists 31
Table 4: Insufficient tourist facilities 31
Table 5: Negative perception and publicity 32
Table 6: Lack of skilled staff 32
Table 7: Infrastructures not being of the required level 33
Table 8: Other challenges 33
Table 9: Improve marketing strategies 34
Table 10: Training of staff and service providers 34
Table 11: Networking and partnership with other stakeholders 35
Table 12: Encouraging local population in Rwanda to visit dark tourism sites 35
Table 13: Improve the variety and accessibility of dark tourism attractions 36
Table 14: Other measures 36

LIST OF FIGURES

Figure 1: Gender of respondents 26
Figure 2: Category of respondent 27
Figure 3: Duration of service in the tourism industry 28

ABSTRACT

The study sought to assess the challenges of promoting dark tourism in Rwanda. The study was guided by three objectives: To find out the dark tourism products in Rwanda; to investigate the challenges of promoting dark tourism in Rwanda and to establish measures that could be adopted to promote dark tourism in Rwanda. To achieve the set objectives, the study used a sample of 43 respondents randomly selected from staff of Rwanda Development Board (RDB), museum/memorial site managers and tour operators. Data was collected by use of questionnaire instrument and summarized in tables and graphs following the objectives of the study and frequencies and percentages were calculated based on the data available. The findings indicated that there are various dark tourism products in Rwanda which included Kigali memorial center, Bisesero, Gatwaro Stadium and Gitesi memorial site. Less effective information dissemination, High cost charged to tourists and Lack of skilled staff are the challenges affecting the promotion of dark tourism. Measures that could be adopted to promote dark tourism in Rwanda are Improving marketing strategies, Training of staff and service providers and improving the variety and accessibility of dark tourism attractions. The study concluded by noting that Identifying the successful practices in management, branding, marketing, and pricing strategies of dark tourism attractions around the world can aid in applying these ideas towards improving the dark tourism industry in Rwanda. The study recommended that since we are living in a global world, using the mass media advertisements, specifically TV, Newspapers or other tourism information brochures is significantly important in attracting more dark tourists.

Key word
- Tourism
- Dark

CHAPTER ONE

INTRODUCTION AND BACKGROUND TO THE STUDY

1.1 Introduction

This chapter introduces the study by giving the background information, statement of the problem, purpose and objective of the study, research questions, significance and scope of the study and finally organization of the study.

1.2 Background to the study

The notion of tourism in general is rather broad. There are numerous types of tourism that are aimed on fulfillment of different customers' needs. Tourism and traveling have become not only a means of satisfaction of spiritual wants, but also most people's life style (Amabile, 2005). For ages people from all over the world were interested in destinations connected with death and suffering of the olds. These places have been attracting people from everywhere long since by the tragic history or shadowy past. Tours devoted to visits of the most tragically places on the planet are becoming more and more popular among tourists from all over the world. For that reason, the notion of dark tourism is becoming more popular among demanding customers. Dark tourism is the act of traveling and visiting sites, attractions and exhibitions which have real or recreated death suffering or the seemingly macabre as the main theme (Stone, 2005). Similarly, Foley and Lennon (1997), whilst adding a chronological element, define dark tourism as the visitation to any site associated with death, disaster and tragedy in the twentieth century for remembrance, education or entertainment. Meanwhile, Tarlow acknowledges historical dimensions and identifies dark tourism as visitations to places where tragedies or historically noteworthy death has occurred and that continue to impact our lives (Tarlow, (2005).

Deaths, disasters and atrocities in touristic form are becoming an increasingly pervasive feature within the contemporary visitor economy. For the individual who wishes to journey and gaze upon real or recreated death, a plethora of sites, attractions and exhibitions are now emerging across the world to cater to the darker side of travel (Sharpley and Stone, 2009). Indeed, seemingly morbid practices within tourism vary from people gazing upon sites of brutality at former World War One battlefields of northern France, to visitors purchasing souvenirs of atrocity at Ground Zero, to tourists sightseeing in the ruins of New Orleans (after Hurricane Katrina), or excursionists touring sites of genocide and tragedy such as Auschwitz-Birkenau or the Killing Fields of Cambodia. Consequently, the phenomenon by which people visit, purposefully or as part of a broader recreational itinerary, the diverse range of sites, attractions and exhibitions that offer a (re)presentation of death and human suffering is ostensibly growing within contemporary society. As a result, the rather emotive label of dark tourism, and its scholarly sister term of than tourism, has entered academic discourse and media parlance Seaton, 1996)

Indeed for many years, humans have been attracted to sites and events that are associated with death, disaster, suffering, violence and killing. From ancient Rome and gladiatorial combat to attendance at public executions, sites of death have held a voyeuristic appeal. Dark tourism has entered the mainstream and is a popular subject of media attention. More importantly it is used as a marketing term on sites such as http://thecabinet.com where the category of dark destinations has been in use since 2006. The appeal of a range of global destinations associated with dark acts shows no signs of abatement. Most recently the enduring appeal has been reinforced in New York, Paris and beyond. The ground zero site now attracts a significantly greater number of visitors since the terrorist attacks of 11 September 2001 (Blair, 2002). In Paris, the death site of Diana, princess of Wales evidenced pilgrimages and visitation following her death and the site of her burial place Althorpe achieved significant visitations for the three years following her death. In Africa, sites in Angola, South Africa, Sierra Leon, and Rwanda have all demonstrated the appeal of dark histories to visitors (Rowe, 2007).

A basic analysis of Rwanda's history shows that there are a number of death related visitor sites or attractions, Rucunshu war grounds, Musanze cave and Rwandan president Juvénal Habyarimana airplane crash at Kanombe are typical dark tourist sites in Rwanda, which are also well known in the world. As anywhere in Africa, pre-colonial Rwanda was not exempt from social unrest and violence. Bernard Lugan talks of revolutions, conquest, and succession wars in Rwanda before colonization, each with its lot of victims. Indeed, just one year before the Germans entered the country in 1897, the king Mibambwe IV Rutalindwa had been assassinated in a bloody coup (1896) and replaced by one of his half-brothers, king Musinga. War of succession known as the Rucunshu war (1896-1897) between king Musinga faction and Rutarindwa faction was so destructive and symbols of that bloody battle are still visible at

Rukaza hill. Musanze cave lies in the grounds about 2km from the town center off the Gisenyi road. The main cave reportedly 2km long has an entrance the size of a cathedral. Legend has it that Musanze cave was created by a local king and that it has been used as a refuge on several occasions in history whereas during the 1994 Massacre it was used as a killing site and recently the place is still littered with human remains. The airplane carrying Rwandan president Juvénal Habyarimana and Burundian president Cyprian Ntaryamira was shot down as it prepared to land in Kigali, Rwanda. The assassination set in motion some of the bloodiest events of the late 20th century, the Rwandan Genocide and the First Congo War. (Prunier, G. 1995)

1.3 Statement of the Problem

The tourism industry is one of the world's fastest growing industries with estimated growth in global travel expanding from 450 million travelers in 1992 to 730 million by the year 2010 (World Tourism Organization, 2006). In the recent world Economic Forum Travel and Tourism Competitive Index, Rwanda is ranked 7th for sub Saharan Africa ahead of its more established East Africa neighbors Kenya and Tanzania. Tourism continues to perform way above average for Rwanda's economy, with a reported 11 percent rise in revenues generated for the first six months of 2012, up from the previous year by nearly 13 million US Dollars to 128.3 million US Dollars (RDB, 2012). Although the tourism industry in Rwanda is the fasting growing, it is surprisingly to note that the country's tourism initiatives currently attract specific tourists, particularly eco-tourists who are drawn to the country's natural attractions, especially the world-famous mountain gorillas. Despite an increasing number of tourists traveling to places of horrific human catastrophe, for example nearly a million tourists visited the Auschwitz-Birkenau Museum in 2005, up from half that the year before, this has not be the case in Rwanda, few tourists are attracted to the dark tourism attractions in Rwanda like genocide memorial sites. There this study intends to assess the challenges of promoting dark tourism in Rwanda.

1.4 Purpose of the study

The purpose of this study was to assess the challenges of promoting dark tourism in Rwanda.

1.4.1 Objectives of the study

a) To find out the dark tourism products in Rwanda.
b) To investigate the challenges of promoting dark tourism in Rwanda.
c) To establish measures that could be adopted to promote dark tourism in Rwanda.

1.4.2 Research questions

a) What are the dark tourism products in Rwanda?
b) What are the challenges of promoting dark tourism in Rwanda?
c) What are the measures that could be adopted to promote dark tourism in Rwanda?

1.5 Scope of the study

Geographical scope
The study was conducted in Rwanda
Content Scope
The study focused on the challenges of promoting dark tourism in Rwanda.

1.6 Significance of the study

The following disciplines could benefit from the findings of the study:
- Dark tourism is a special type of tourism business which does not appeal to everyone but has an important role in delivering information and bringing the past to present. Therefore this study would help the government of Rwanda, tourism planners, managers, promoters and advocators to figure out the potential dark tourism market needs and advancements define target groups and implement conductive market penetration strategies.
- The study would be useful for future researchers interested in carrying out research in the field concerned with tourism that is why a copy would be handed over in the library.

- Finally, the study would be of great importance to the researcher due to the broad knowledge and understanding that would be achieved from the research especially in the field of Tourism management and development.

The research would also be able to fulfil some of the requirements for the award of bachelor's degree in travel and tourism management

1.7 Structure of the dissertation

The research project composed of five sections: Chapter 1 introduced the study by giving the background information of the study, research problem, objectives, significance, scope and structure of the study. Chapter 2 will cover the literature review. Chapter 3 concentrated on discussing the research methodology adopted for the study and relevant justifications. It outlined the methodology for carrying out the secondary and primary data collections and how results were analyzed. Chapter 4 dealt with data analysis, interpretation of the result, in this chapter, the researcher analyzed and interpreted the data in order to fulfill the objectives of the study and presented the data pertaining to the problem. The final chapter formed the discussion, conclusion and gave recommendations as to the next steps needed to help transform Rwanda's dark tourism industry.

CHAPTER TWO

LITERATURE REVIEW

2.0 Introduction

In this section the researcher described and explained the concepts and theories that are relevant in the field of dark tourism in order to give a comprehensive analysis and understanding of the research topic.

2.1 Definition and explanation of key terms

2.1.1 Tourism

Generally, there are several common assumptions about tourism. Mathieson and Wall define tourism as: the temporary movement of people to destinations outside their normal places of work and residence, the activities undertaken during their stay in those destinations and the facilities created to care to their need (Mathieson and Wall 1982). Similarly, for Buckart and Medlik, tourism denotes the temporary short term movement of people to destinations outside the places where they normally live (Buckart and Medlik, 1974). The geographers Shaw and Williams adopted the formal definition by international organizations, such as the World Tourism Office, that tourism includes all travel that involves a stay of at least one night, but less than one year, away from home (Shaw and Williams, 1994). This definition pointed out that the purpose of traveling may include visiting friends and relatives, or working on a business trip. In the lecture of Business Tourism and Travel Management Course in Savonia UAS, Kuopio, Finalnd, the definition of tourism was shown as temporal short term movement of people to destination outside the places where they normally live and work, and activities during their stay at these destinations; it includes movement for all purposes, as well as day visits and excursions. (Verhela, 2011)

2.1.2 Dark Tourism

Dark Tourism is also called as black tourism or grief tourism which is not a very new activity or phenomenon in nowadays tourism market, including castles and battle fields, sites of natural or manmade disaster and the prisons that open to public. The term of dark tourism was first coined by two researchers, Malcolm Foley and J. John Lennon, as a means of describing, the phenomenon which encompasses the presentation and consumption (by visitors) of real and commoditized death and disaster sites (Foley and Lennon 1996). A large number of sites associated with war, genocide, assassination and other tragic events have become significant tourist destinations, Lennon and Foley call this phenomenon dark tourism (Lennon and Foley 2000). The authors even refine this definition further by noting the actions which do and do not consist of dark tourism. For example, the behavior of friends and families visiting the dark tourism sites cannot be categorized as dark tourism. In their book, Lennon and Foley define dark tourism referring to events that have occurred in recent times, which force the visitor to question modernity. Lennon and Foley see dark tourism as the commoditization of anxiety and doubt. (Lennon and Foley, 2002) The University of Central Lancashire undertook the academic research into dark tourism. They say: Dark tourism is the act of travel and visitation to sites, attractions and exhibitions which have real or recreated death, suffering or the seemingly macabre as a main theme. (Kendle, 2006). From The Baltic Times, they say: Dark tourism is a different type of tourist attraction; it is the act of travel and visitation to sites of death, disaster and the seemingly macabre. Tourists flock to experience sites of past terror that offer up grim and disturbing tragedies. (Webber, 2007)

2.2 Theoretical Overview of Dark Tourism

Indeed, for as long as people have been able to travel they have been drawn, purposefully or otherwise, towards sites, attractions or events that are linked in one way or another with disaster, suffering, violence or death (Stone, 2005). The gladiatorial games of the Roman era, pilgrimages, or attendance at medieval public executions were for example early forms of such death related tourism as Boorstin alleges, the first guided tour in England was a rail trip to witness the hanging of two murderers. The tour was arranged in Cornwall in 1838 to take people of Wade bridge by special train to the nearby town of Bodmin. There they witnessed the hanging of two murderers and since the Bodmin gallows were in clear sight of the uncovered station, excursionists had their fun without even leaving the open railway carriages (Boorstin, 1964). In the specific context of warfare, however, Seaton (1999) observes that death, suffering and tourism have been related for centuries (also Smith, 1998; Knox, 2006), citing tourism to the battlefield of Waterloo from 1816 onwards as a notable nineteenth century example of what he terms than tourism. Additionally, in the nineteenth century, visits to morgues were as McConnell (1989) notes, a regular feature of tours of Paris perhaps a forerunner to the Body Worlds exhibitions in London, Los Angeles, Tokyo and elsewhere that since the late 1990s have attracted visitors in their tens of thousands (Body Worlds, 2008). Similarly, the historical precedent of visitors gazing upon the less fortunate in society, similar to Brazilian favelas slum tours of today was set by Jack London's 1903 sociological treatise about the abject poverty of London at the turn of the 20th century. In his commentary of social and political failure, The People of the Abyss', an affluent Edwardian descends into the slums and gazes at the underworld. (Rolfes, 2010)

As considered shortly, the extent to which dark tourism may be considered an historical phenomenon that is applicable to sites, attractions or events that pre-date living memory remains a subject of debate (Wight, 2006; Seaton, 2009). It is clear, however, that visitors have long been attracted to places or events associated in one way or another with death, disaster and suffering. Equally, there can be little doubt that, over the last half century and commensurate with the remarkable growth in tourism more generally, dark tourism has become both widespread and diverse. In terms of supply there has been a rapid growth in the provision of such attractions or experiences. Indeed there appears to be an increasing number of people keen to promote or profit from dark events as tourist attractions, such as the Pennsylvania farmer who offered a $65 per person Flight 93 Tour to the crash site of the United Airlines Flight 93 one of the hijacked aircraft on 9/11 (Bly, 2003; Sharpley, 2005). Moreover, dark tourism has become more widely recognized as both a form of tourism and a promotional tool with websites, such as www.thecabinet.com, listing numerous dark tourism sites around the world (Dark Destinations, 2007). Similarly, a recent online poll commissioned by the Czech Tourist Board sought to discover and thus promote the top ten darkest places of interest within the Czech Republic. (Sindelaova, 2008)

At the same time, there is evidence of a greater willingness or desire on the part of tourists to visit dark attractions and in particular sites of death. For example, in August 2002, local residents in the small Cambridge shire town of Soham in the UK appealed for an end to the so called grief tourism that was bringing tens of thousands of visitors to their area. Many of these visitors traveling from all over Britain had come to lay flowers, to light candles in the local church or to sign books of condolence. Others had simply come to gaze at the community, indeed it was reported that tourist buses en route to Cambridge or nearby Ely Cathedral were making detours through the town (O'Neill, 2002). All however, had been drawn to Soham by its association with a terrible and highly publicized crime: the abduction and murder of two young schoolgirls. In the same year Ground Zero in New York attracted three and a half million visitors almost double the number that annually visited the observation platform of the World Trade Centre prior to 9/11 (Blair, 2002). Interestingly, repeating what had occurred at Asbury Park with the SS Morro Castle disaster, the site also attracted numerous street vendors selling trinkets that run the gamut of taste (Vega, 2002). Kitsch souvenirs on sale ranged from framed photographs of the burning towers to Osama Bin Laden toilet paper, his picture printed on each square (Lisle, 2004). More generally, evidence suggests contemporary tourists are increasingly traveling to destinations associated with death and suffering. According to one recent report, for example, places such as Rwanda, Sierra Leone, Angola and Afghanistan are experiencing a significant upsurge in tourism demand. (Rowe, 2007)

Nevertheless, despite the long history and increasing contemporary evidence of travel to sites or attractions associated with death, it is only relatively and perhaps surprisingly recently that academic attention has been focused upon what has collectively been referred to as dark tourism (Foley and Lennon, 1996). More specifically the publication of Lennon and Foley's (2000) *Dark Tourism: The Attraction of Death and Disaster* introduced the term to a wider audience, stimulating a significant degree of academic interest and debate. Consequently, understanding of the phenomenon of dark tourism remains limited, (though a new book on dark tourism by Sharpley and Stone (2009) goes some way to addressing this issue). Many commentators explore and analyze specific manifestations of dark tourism. These range from war museums which adopt both traditional and contemporary museology methods of representation (Wight and Lennon, 2004), to genocide commemoration visitor sites and the political ideology attached to such remembrance. (Williams, 2004)

2.3 Dark Tourism Products

Drawing upon issues and concepts, various types of visitor sites, attractions, and exhibitions have emerged; the study has compiled a conceptual classification that reflects the current composition of dark tourism supply. Seven fundamental types of dark tourism are identified with their relative position on the Dark Tourism Spectrum model. (Stone, 2006)

2.3.1 Dark Fun Factories

A Dark Fun Factory alludes to those visitor sites, attractions and tours that predominately have an entertainment focus and commercial ethic, and which present recreated or fictional death and macabre events. Indeed, these types of products possess a high degree of tourism infrastructure, are purposeful in their design and are in essence fun centric. Consequently, this classification of dark tourism may occupy the lightest edges of the dark tourism spectrum. Dark Fun Factories offer sanitized products in terms of representation and are perhaps perceived as less authentic. For instance, the Dungeon concepts now being rolled out across Europe by Merlin Entertainments Ltd is a classic Dark Fun Factory. Perhaps most famous of the Dungeon attractions, the London Dungeon has long drawn visitors to its doors with the promise of ghouls and displays of morbidity. With gruesome and highly visual, yet family friendly exhibits portraying less savory aspects of (past) life, such as the Black Death or Jack the Ripper, the London Dungeon offers a socially acceptable environment in which to gaze upon simulated death and associated suffering (Stone, 2006).

2.3.2 Dark Exhibitions

Dark Exhibitions refer to those exhibitions and sites that essentially blend the product design to reflect education and potential learning opportunities. With a Dark Fun Factory offering a commercial and more entertainment based product, Dark Exhibitions offer products or experiences which revolve around death, suffering or the macabre, and which often possess an inherent commemorative, educational and reflective message. Dark Exhibitions are manifested within an eclectic product range and are often located away from the actual site of death or macabre event. Indeed, the multitude of museums that display death and associated suffering with an educative or commemorative focus may be classed as Dark Exhibitions. For instance, the

Smithsonian Museum of American History recently constructed an exhibit that displayed images and artifacts of the September 11 terrorist attacks under a banner of capturing history and instilling a sense of veneration for the victims. (Robinson2003)

2.3.3 Dark Dungeons

Dark Dungeons refer to those sites and attractions that present bygone penal and justice codes to the present day consumer and subsequently revolve around former prisons and Courthouses. These product types essentially have a combination of entertainment and education as a main merchandise focus, possess a relatively high degree of commercialism and tourism infrastructure and occupy sites that were originally non purposeful for dark tourism. For instance, the Galleries of Justice visitor attraction based in Nottingham UK, suggests in its marketing literature that it is the only site in the country where you could be arrested, sentenced and executed (Galleries of Justice, 2005). Promoted as the Family Attraction of the Year under marketing strap line Feel the Fear, the Galleries of Justice site is created from buildings originally used as prisons and courts from the 1780's until as recently as the 1980's. With a representation of harsh penal codes from days gone by, the attraction seeks to entertain the visitor through heritage promoting educational and historical content.

With regards to Strange and Kempa's (2003) analysis of shades of dark tourism, Robben Island, the former prison of Nelson Mandela located off the Cape Town coast in South Africa is inextricably linked to the struggle against colonialism, the fight for freedom, democracy and peace in South Africa. Indeed the South African government stated whilst putting forward Robben Island as a World Heritage Site that the site should be turned around into a source of enlightenment and education on the dangers of myopic philosophies and social and economic practices whose primary and sole objective is the oppression of one group by another (Government of South Africa, 1999). Therefore, with a desire to represent the struggle for social justice, and for Robben Island to act as a symbol of freedom, the fundamental product design of this Dark Dungeon is that of education. Yet, as Shackley notes, Robben Island is part theme park, part shrine and part museum and a location with the potential to make a great deal of money. (Shackley 2001)

2.3.4 Dark Resting Places

Dark Resting Places focuses upon the cemetery or grave markers as potential products for dark tourism (Seaton, 2002). Consequently the cemetery within contemporary society acts as a romanticized if not rather macabre urban regeneration tool. In particular tourism planners often use the cemetery as a mechanism to promote visitation to an area, conserve the structural integrity of landscape and architecture and sustain the ecology of local environments (Meyer and Peters, 2001). With an increasing infrastructure being built around these Dark Resting Places mainly through association groups, the use of the internet and dedicated guide tours, the cemetery is fast becoming a place where the living are charmed by the dead and thus may be plotted left of centre on the Dark Tourism Spectrum with both dark and light characteristics. Indeed, according to the Association of Significant Cemeteries in Europe (ASCE), cemeteries are an integral component of cultural heritage and those cemeteries with historical or artistic significance should be conserved (ASCE, 2005).

For instance, the famous Pere Lachaise cemetery is the largest park in Paris and attracts over two million visitors a year and beyond its primary function of interment the cemetery has evolved into an open air museum and pantheon garden (Northstar Gallery, 1998). On a less grand scale is the development of Weaste Cemetery in Salford, UK. As part of a wider urban regeneration programme, local tourism planners are attempting to amalgamate history and ecology as distinct product features and to encourage visitation to this Dark Resting Place. Salford City Council states: Weaste Cemetery is primarily a place to respect and commemorate the loved ones we have lost. People also visit cemeteries for exercise and relaxation, and to study nature and local history. It is our aim to offer a fitting environment for the bereaved and also to enhance the life of the community. (Salford City Council, 2004)

2.3.5 Dark Shrines

Dark Shrines are those sites that trade on the act of remembrance and respect for the recently deceased. Hence, Dark Shrines are often constructed formally or informally, very close to the site of death and within a very short period of the death occurring. Additionally, these types of events dominate the media agenda for relatively short periods of time hence attaching a higher level of political awareness and influence to a particular Dark Shrine site during the media period. Dark Shrines offer a semi permanent and tangible focal point for the bereaved. Indeed, most Dark Shrines are non purposeful for tourism and thus possess very little tourism infrastructure due to their temporal nature. For example, the Dark Shrine, which was constructed in the now usual floral edifice around the gates of Kensington Palace at the time Diana, Princess of Wales was killed in 1997, became a focal point for millions of people. Yet, within a relatively short period this Dark Shrine had been dismantled and reconstructed at Althorp House, the site of Diana's internment. Interestingly, more than a decade after her death, the business of remembering Diana is doing well, with tourism infrastructure at Althorp House evolving to include award winning exhibitions illustrating Diana's death and subsequent tributes. (Merrin, 1999)

2.3.6 Dark Conflict Sites

Smith (1998) suggests that activities, sites or destinations associated with warfare are a major component of the wider tourist attraction market. Thus this category termed here Dark Conflict Sites, revolves around war and battlefields and their commodification as potential tourism products. Indeed, Dark Conflict Sites are increasingly becoming more commercialized and as a result have an increasing tourism infrastructure. For instance in terms of formalized infrastructure a number of dedicated tour operators now offer trips to various battlefields either specifically or as part of a wider holiday itinerary. These tours, which essentially bring organized violence back to life often focus upon battlefields of World War One. Indeed the Western Front Battlefield Tours organization offer the discerning visitor an opportunity to tour battle sites such as Ypres and the Somme in small groups complete with trench maps, war diaries and in depth commentary (Western Front Battlefield Tours, 2005). With the recent opening of a purpose built visitor centre near the Memorial of the Missing at Thiepval in northern France the business of remembrance has taken on a more structured focus.

World War One tour products are well established, other Dark Conflict Sites are beginning to realize their dark tourism potential. For example the area in the Solomon Islands where the Battle of Guadalcanal was fought during World War Two may become an established site on future holiday itineraries. Along with stunning paradise beaches, many of the islands and the surrounding seas are still littered with the detritus of war, something the government and local businessmen have realized is a potential tourism goldmine. (Squires, 2004)

2.3.7 Dark Camps of Genocide

Dark Camps of Genocide represents those sites and places which have genocide, atrocity and catastrophe as the main product theme and thus occupy the darkest edges of the dark tourism spectrum. Mercifully, genocide sites are not particularly common but do exist in places such as Rwanda, Cambodia, and Kosovo. Dark Camps of Genocide are produced to provide the ultimate emotional experience whereby visitors sightsee in the mansions of the dead (Keil, 2005). With a product message designed around education and commemoration and unlike Dark Exhibitions being located at the actual site of the death event, Dark Camps of Genocide tell the terrible tales of human suffering and infliction and consequently have a high degree of political ideology attached to them. Thus Dark Camps of Genocide are those sites that mark a concentration of death and atrocity and a concentration of death is no more apparent than that committed throughout the Holocaust. Hence, Auschwitz-Birkenau now a visitor site and example of a Dark Camp of Genocide represents most the Holocaust for the scale of atrocities committed there. (Gilbert, 1986)

2.4 The Motivations of Dark Tourism

Most tourists get two main functions and effectiveness from the tourism: education and entertainment. For dark tourism, there is a trend less entertainment and more education. Not every dark tourism site can bring tourists both enjoyment and education; in Budapest dark tourism of House of Terror and Memento Park, tourists can get both, however, like Auschwitz in Poland, most tourists more appreciate for the function of education and enlightenment from their chosen dark tourism. Dark tourism motivations are murky and difficult to unravel: a mix of reverence and thrill of coming into close proximity with death. Over half a million people visit Auschwitz Birkenau each year. The standard two-and-a-half-hour guided tour gives an audience at best an abridged understanding of this vast and sprawling site. But from the dark tourism, more and more people get education, edification and enlightenment from the real history, especially for the topic relevant to the life and death. (Lennon and Foley, 2000)

As Tarlow suggested, dark tourism has the commercial function which changes the horrors of yesterday to the business of today. In this viewpoint, dark tourism sites are not only the places for visitors to show respect to the victims, but also the tourists points for get business benefits. (Tarlow 2005)

Dark tourism is an increasingly widespread feature in the popular culture landscape. Making absent death present may help the individual to understand mortality. *"We see death, but we do not touch it"* (Tercier, 2005). Even though people are spectators to more deaths than any previous generations were, thanks to technological development, it is argued that the individual is left isolated in the face of death and, as mentioned before, without enough craved information. Therefore, dark tourism offers a way for an individual to indulge curiosity in a socially acceptable environment and in that way it gives an opportunity to construct one's own contemplations of mortality. (Stone and Sharpley, 2008)

In addition, visiting a dark attraction can be a very educational experience by raising awareness of terrible events of the past, dark tourism guides human to understand the world. While much of modern tourism is simply about recreation, visiting a dark attraction can be a multi dimensional experience that can have a deep impact on your life. (Daams, 2007) For example, Reiss (2009) compares his visits in the National Civil Rights Museum (Memphis, USA) and the House of Terror and describes the House of Terror as *"an artistic and educational triumph"* compared with the NCRM. Reiss continues revealing that a visit in the House of Terror encouraged him to read more about Hungarian history and evoked an appreciation of the plight of the Hungarians. Experiencing the absent death becoming present may help minimize the threat of the inevitable and increasing acceptance of mortality. It allows individuals to view their own death as distant and with hope of a good death. (Stone and Sharpley 2008)

Dark sites can be used as the pretext to explain the current political situation. Visitors are expected to learn from the past and to carry the message forward in order to avoid history happening again. (Tarlow, 2005). A founder and editor of Brave New Traveler, Ian Mackenzie writes in article "The Case of Documenting Death" about his experience of visiting the Killing Fields of Cambodia, known for its history of genocide, famine and death. He describes a moment when he was photographing the scene:

"A part of me felt like a crass tourist, simply collecting photographs just like any other scene, But another side of me felt compelled to bear witness, fulfilling the solemn duty of the traveler to collect evidence of sorrow in order to share it with their friends and family". When a survived victim was telling a true story about the time in work camp, Mackenzie was listening in disbelief

and unable to understand such sadness. For the victims presenting the past is a way to share the story and remind the listener not to make the same mistakes again. (Mackenzie, 2007)

2.4.1 Strategies used in promoting/marketing dark tourism

In Vietnam, current governments have promoted war tourism using message of solidarity, a heroic struggle against outside aggressors. At the Cu Chi Tunnel complex where Vietcong ran supplies to forces in South Vietnam, certain interpretations appear geared specifically towards locals. Although some film footage at the visitors centre is original, certain sections depict the rustic atmosphere and local heroes who were honored as 'Number One American Killers. Henderson, (2000)

Numerous brochures of dark tourism sites offer artifacts in their marketing campaigns. At the National Civil Rights Museum in Memphis, you can walk into a Montgomery city bus or a Greyhound bus similar to those used in the 1961 Freedom Rides (National Civil Rights Museum 2002). You can see the salvaged mast of the USS Maine, sunk in 1898, at Arlington National Cemetery in Virginia, (Arlington National Cemetery 2002). At The Second World War Experience Centre in Leeds, England, you can see wartime letters, diaries, photographs, and official papers. The Second World War Experience Centre (2000)

According to MacCannell (1976 and 1989), mechanically reproducing dark tourism sites or objects elevates them as significant touristic attractions. The media played, and still plays, an important role in these reproductions, ranging from Hollywood blockbusters to comic strips. Seaton concurs, "The sustained reproduction of Waterloo through the printed word and graphic image was one of the reasons it achieved a unique place in public imagination" (Seaton, 1999)

Using MacCannell's 5-step process, Seaton (1999) demonstrated the sacralization of the site of the Battle of Waterloo. The *naming* of the battle Waterloo, gave that specific site preeminence and therefore a recognition factor to the public at large. Since the name sounded familiar, it must therefore be important. The *framing and elevation* of Waterloo followed with the erection of monuments and markers to the fallen. With something concrete to now gaze at, tourists began to arrive. Phase three, *enshrinement,* came with an unimportant church rebuilt after the battle. While the artifacts inside the church are still important attractions, people now come to see the building itself. Finally, *mechanical and social reproductions* of Waterloo are still prevalent in society. Guidebooks continue to direct tourists to the site while pubs, streets, and cities can be found across the British Commonwealth. Seaton (1999)

The media also has undeniable influence over pubic interpretation of the landscape including sites of dark tourism. According to Lennon and Foley, global communication technologies are inherent in both the events which are associated with a dark tourism product and are present in the representation of the events for visitors at the site itself. Hence, the relationship between dark tourism and the media is thoroughly interconnected. The 1912 sinking of the *Titanic* is considered to be the genesis of global media. Although television did not exist and communications were slower than today, newspapers and newsreels were quick to report on the tragedy. Forty-six years later, the media again brought the *Titanic* to the forefront of public consciousness with the release of the film, A *Night to Remember.* The film effectively turned the relatively impersonal and largely forgotten sinking into a series of individual's stories of fictional characters upon the vessel. In 1998, the *Titanic* once again raised onto the big screen with the release James Cameron's *Titanic.* (Lennon and Foley 2000)

Modern media not only plays a role in disseminating information to the public off-site (thereby pushing visitors to the destination); it also plays an important role in the development of on-site interpretation (hence pulling visitors). Sites associated with the Kennedy assassination and the US Holocaust Memorial Museum in Washington, D.C. all exemplifies this reliance on media for their interpretation. Lennon and Foley note that central to interpretation at the Sixth Floor Museum are pictorial images including, Upwards of four hundred photographs, and six documentary films (heavily based on contemporary TV coverage) (Lennon and Foley 2000). As a result, since its opening in 1989 the museum has been presented with numerous awards for its use of video. (Zelizer 1992)

2.4.2 Challenges in marketing/ promoting dark tourism

The survival of a dark tourism industry relies heavily on the existence of a tourism culture which allows for an enthusiastic approach to travel by the local population. In many nations, this culture is still absent. Policies regarding dark tourism tend to be makeshift and informal and do not have long term strategies in place, making sustainable growth impossible. Most tourism policies are generally biased towards the development of ecotourism and this bias, termed the

'Northern Bias' by Ghimire is what deters the creation of possible dark tourism initiatives. Ghimire (2001)

In order to allow for the advancement of dark tourism, governments must have existing information on how the industry has grown so far. Yet, while the importance of dark tourism has been widely acknowledged, significant research and information on the current role of dark tourism is still lacking. This is a major constraint to the growth of dark tourism, and this gap stems from the fact that most countries view dark tourism as secondary to attracting the tourism market. As a result, there are very few records of dark tourism initiatives; most governments have put significant effort into promoting ecotourism and tend to find dark tourism particularly in developing countries, to be less important. This is a continuing trend in developing countries and hinders the progress of a viable dark tourism industry. (Ghimire, 2001

Dark tourism is often regarded as being less profit generating to the national economy if compared to ecotourism since it does not generate enough revenue since the volumes of dark tourists if compared to eco tourists are low in some countries. This is due to lack of awareness and understanding by visitors of the excellent dark tourism destination in a country and the range of accommodation options and attractions available. Lack of resources and significant financial, cultural and infrastructural obstacles also hamper efforts aimed at promoting dark tourism, which would lead to a self sustaining industry. (Poirier, 2000)

Notwithstanding the undoubted impact of technology on the distribution and delivery of dark tourism services, people remain a critical dimension within the successful delivery of dark tourism services. The story of successful dark tourism enterprises is one that is largely about people; how they are recruited, how they are managed, how they are trained and educated, how they are valued and rewarded, and how they are supported through a process of continuous learning and career development. In today's tourism environment, worldwide, the pressing issues facing the dark tourism sector relate to a combination of recruitment and retention; labor turnover; skills shortages; training and development opportunities; and workplace conditions. Baum, (2007)

Dealing with the past is a laborious task as sufferings of real people are involved and not everyone accepts that stories about atrocities should be told to tourists just for the sake of entertainment. Charging money for telling horrible and macabre stories is also believed to be wrong by many, as grief is transformed into a commodity just to please the increasing number of tourists. Apart from that, dark tourism is very susceptible to poor tourism infrastructure, and bad press publicity. Besides, the intense competition for especially with similar products like eco tourism affects the dark tourism sector performance. (Shackley, 2001)

2.5 Rwanda Tourism industry

Rwanda's fascinating history, its distinct culture and varied natural attractions come together to form a unique experience for any type of tourist. Over the past eleven years in particular, the country has transformed itself into an interesting destination with rich experiences for any visitor. With an infectious enthusiasm, Booth and Briggs describe it as a vibrant, safe and energetic nation well able to tackle the demands of the 21st century and to welcome tourists. This enthusiasm for Rwanda's tourism was not always the case, as the orientation was different, but since 1994, the industry has undergone a significant overhaul, not the least of which was that Rwanda had to strategically try to establish itself as a unique destination in Africa, especially being a small country and neighboring important African tourist destinations like Uganda, Kenya and Tanzania. Rwanda's tourism has mainly been based on its natural endowments which coincided with conservation and preservation efforts. (Booth and Briggs, 2004)

2.5.1 Dark Tourism in Rwanda

A basic analysis of Rwanda's history shows that there are a number of death related visitor sites or attractions, Rucunshu war grounds, Musanze cave and Rwandan president Juvénal Habyarimana airplane crash at Kanombe are typical dark tourist sites in Rwanda, which are also well known in the world. As anywhere in Africa, pre-colonial Rwanda was not exempt from social unrest and violence. Bernard Lugan talks of revolutions, conquest, and succession wars in Rwanda before colonization, each with its lot of victims. Indeed, just one year before the Germans entered the country in 1897, the king Mibambwe IV Rutalindwa had been assassinated in a bloody coup (1896) and replaced by one of his half-brothers, king Musinga. War of succession known as the Rucunshu war (1896-1897) between king Musinga faction and Rutarindwa faction was so destructive and symbols of that bloody battle are still visible at Rukaza hill. Musanze cave lies in the grounds about 2km from the town center Musanze off the Gisenyi road. The main cave reportedly 2km long has an entrance the size of a cathedral. Legend has it that Musanze cave was created by a local king and that it has been used as a refuge on several occasions in history whereas during the 1994 Massacre it was used as a killing site and recently the place is still littered with human remains. The airplane carrying Rwandan president Juvénal Habyarimana and Burundian president Cyprian Ntaryamira was shot down as it prepared to land in Kigali, Rwanda. The assassination set in motion some of the bloodiest events of the late 20th century, the Rwandan Genocide and the First Congo War. (Prunier, G. 1995)

Because of its particularly violent past, Rwanda has become a symbol and of the enduring effects of bloodshed. For several years, the genocide in Rwanda has attracted the attention of scholars, researchers, world leaders, and even Hollywood celebrities. While it has become the object of numerous studies on genocide and human suffering, Rwanda remains, as Halilovich points out, first and foremost a private tragedy of the survivors who lost their closest family members in 1994 (Halilovich 2007). Thus, besides having a historical and cultural link, genocide Memorial sites and museums established on the territories where the crime of genocide was committed against thousands of people in 1994 are symbolical representation of the atrocity committed there. The Memorial sites are also a space where the identity of some of the deceased has been partially reconstructed by displaying various belongings found at the scene, and forensically collected and preserved to be seen by curious visitors. Over the last few years, the Memorial sites and its surroundings have been frequently visited not only by scholars, but also by tourists who have been attracted to this 'beautiful and touching place'. (Honig and Wagner, 2008)

The purpose of the memorial centers and museums is two-fold: preserving the memory of the dead, but also reminding people of those who survived the genocide. There are two main areas within the memorial centers that symbolically illuminate the darkness; shedding light on the lives that are gone, but also on the lives of survivors. Some of them have a cinema projector and a few benches where visitors can sit and watch a short documentary film, *Rwanda, April 1994*, a combination of authentic footage from the day Rwanda fell and narratives by a few survivors of the genocide. The film tells a powerful story, allowing survivors to speak about their everyday struggle to come to terms with losing their loved ones and surviving in post-genocide Rwanda. The film simultaneously tells the story of the dead and of the living, reminding the visitors that the dead are still present in the everyday lives of surviving families. (UK 1999)

2.6 Chapter Two Summary

Generally, there are several common assumptions about tourism. Mathieson and Wall define tourism as: the temporary movement of people to destinations outside their normal places of work and residence, the activities undertaken during their stay in those destinations and the facilities created to care to their need, (Mathieson and Wall 1982). The term of dark tourism was first coined by two researchers, Malcolm Foley and J. John Lennon, as a means of describing, the phenomenon which encompasses the presentation and consumption (by visitors) of real and commoditized death and disaster sites (Foley and Lennon 1996). A large number of sites associated with war, genocide, assassination and other tragic events have become significant tourist destinations. Indeed, for as long as people have been able to travel they have been drawn, purposefully or otherwise, towards sites, attractions or events that are linked in one way or another with disaster, suffering, violence or death (Stone, 2005).

Drawing upon issues and concepts, various types of visitor sites, attractions, and exhibitions have emerged; seven fundamental types of dark tourism are identified with their relative position on the Dark Tourism Spectrum model. (Stone, 2006); Dark Fun Factories, Dark Exhibitions, Dark Dungeons, Dark Resting Places, Dark Shrines, Dark Conflict Sites and Dark Camps of Genocide. Most tourists get two main functions and effectiveness from the tourism: education and entertainment. For dark tourism, there is a trend less entertainment and more education.

According to MacCannell (1976 and 1989), mechanically reproducing dark tourism sites or objects elevates them as significant touristic attractions. The media played, and still plays, an important role in these reproductions, ranging from Hollywood blockbusters to comic strips. However, the survival of a dark tourism industry relies heavily on the existence of a tourism culture which allows for an enthusiastic approach to travel by the local population. In many nations, this culture is still absent.

Because of its particularly violent past, Rwanda has become a symbol and of the enduring effects of bloodshed. For several years, the genocide in Rwanda has attracted the attention of scholars, researchers, world leaders, and even Hollywood celebrities. (Halilovich 2007)

CHAPTER THREE

RESEARCH METHODOLOGY

This chapter presents the elements of methodology that was applied in the study. The chapter covered research design, area of study, population of the study, sample size, sampling procedure, data collection methods and instruments, procedure for data collection and data analysis;

3.1 Research Design

The study followed a qualitative and quantitative research model. The researcher used questionnaire to a large sample of population and was therefore intended to find facts which relate to field of study. Hence a survey method of data collection using questionnaire was used.

3.3 Study population

(Dooley 1995) defines a study population as the collection of all individual units or respondents to whom the results of a survey are to be generalized. This definition suggests the close association between the concept and the surveys. A population is an entire aggregation or eligible group from which a sample can be drawn. The target population is the aggregate of cases about which the researcher would like to make generalizations (Polit and Beck, 2004).

Therefore Target population of this study was 46 respondents selected from tour operators, museum/memorial site managers and RDB staff

3.4 Sample size

Burns (1995) consider sample as any part of a population, Dooley (1995) restrict it the portion of the population selected for study. It is a subset of the population from which a generalization about the population is made. This means that the sample selected should represent most characteristics of the population so that it can be considered representative of the population. According to (Polit and Hungler 1989), sampling refers to the process of selecting a portion of the population to represent the entire population.

According to (Kenneth D. Bailey 1994) a sample is sub set or portion of the total population under study.

The sample of the respondents for this study was 34 tour operators, 11 museum/memorial site managers (Kandt House Museum of Natural History, Kigali Genocide Memorial Centre, National Museum of Rwanda, Rwesero Art Museum, Ukari Inyanza,) and 1 RDB staff.

3.5 Sampling procedure

In determining the sample, Simple random sampling was used to select the tour operators that were used in the study. The researcher picked all 34 tour operator around Kigali city and considered them to participate in the study. The study involved all 34 tour operators because the researcher wanted to solicit a very high response rate that provides more reliable results.

On the other hand, 8 managers of the museum and memorial sites, plus 1 RDB staff were purposively selected to participate in the study. They were purposively selected because they were aware of the challenges of promoting dark tourism in Rwanda.

This table shows the number of respondents:

Respondents	Population	Number of respondents	Percentages %
Museum & memorial sites	11	8	19
Tour operators	34	34	79
RDB staff	1	1	2
Total	**46**	**43**	**100**

3.6 Data Collection Instruments

Data was collected using different instruments. Hence use of:-

3.6.1 Questionnaires

The researcher employed self administered questionnaires which are as Bailey (1994) noted instruments of data collection that are handed out to respondents and are filled by them without any assistance from the interviewer.

The researchers chose this instrument because he wanted to cover a large representative sample of **43** respondents who included tour operators, RDB staff and managers As Cano (2000) observed, self- administered questionnaires are cheaper to use and can be distributed on a large scale. In addition, sensitive topics, like the one covered by the researcher, could only be effectively studied or examined using questionnaires. Furthermore, standardized questionnaires used by in this study eliminated interviewer bias and solicited a very high response rate as Bernard (2006) had observed.

The questionnaires were semi-structured and were open ended. To ease the processing of data, options for answers were provided where applicable.

3.6.2 Documentation

The study reviewed various document of RDB in order to obtain secondary data. Such information related to dark tourism and it was obtained from such documents as reports.

3.7 Procedure for Data Collection

The researcher communicated to the Human Resources Department of selected tour operators and RDB to seek authority to access employees. The researcher explained that the information provided was purely for research purposes.

Self-administered questionnaires were given out personally by the researcher to the selected sample. There was a scale regarding the answers provided against which a respondent would only tick one that bare close relation to the question asked in the questionnaire.

3.8 Data Management and Analysis

3.8.1 Qualitative analysis

Qualitative data was be edited, coded and analyzed using themes derived from the objectives of the study which were dark tourism products in Rwanda; challenges to the promotion of dark tourism; measure to the challenges of dark tourism.

3.8.2 Quantitative analysis

The data collected was checked and edited for clarity, legibility, relevance and adequacy. This involved checking for non-response and acceptance or rejection of answers, which had been pre-coded by the researcher. These codes eased the process of data entry. The data was cleaned, tabulated and weighted and percentages were used to analyze the data.

3.8 Ethical Issues

Ethical issues in this research were concern, among other things, maintaining confidentiality about the information gathered from respondents, using secured data for academic purposes only and ensuring that the respondents' personalities are not exploited.

CHAPTER FOUR

DATA ANALYSIS AND PRESENATATION

4.0 Introduction

This chapter presents findings, analysis and interpretation of data collected in the field. The interpretation, discussion and assessment of the data were carried out in relation to the objectives of the study and to present the findings, the researcher has used figures and tables.

4.1 Background information of respondents

A belief personal profile of respondents is provided in this section. This information was obtained from section A of the questionnaire. Personal information includes respondent's gender, category of respondent and duration of service in the tourism industry.

Figure 1: Gender of respondents

Respondents' distribution according to gender is shown in figure 1 below;

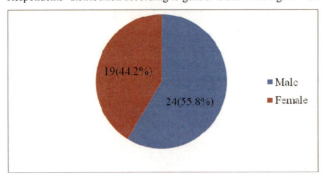

Source: The researcher 2012

The results in figure 1 above showed that 44.2% of the respondents were female and 55.8% male. This indicated that both male and female respondents were represented in the study

Figure 2: Category of respondent

Respondents' distribution according to Category is shown in figure 2 below;

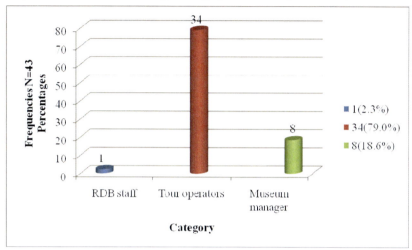

Source: The researcher 2012

Findings in figure 2 showed that 79.0% of the respondents were tour operators well as 18.6% were museum and memorial site managers and 2.3% RDB staff. This is an indication all categories were represented in the study hence the results are not biased.

Figure 3: Duration of service in the tourism industry

Respondent's duration of service in the tourism industry is shown in figure 3 below;

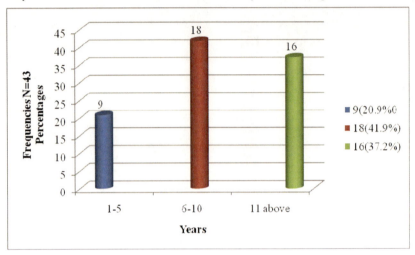

Source: The researcher 2012

Figure 3, results indicates that the majority of respondents 41.9% had experience of between 6-10 years and 37.2% had 1-5 years experience well as 20.9% had experience of more than 11 years. This is an indication that all the respondents had experience of more than one year in the tourism industry and therefore exposed to and familiar with the tourism industry.

4.2 THE DARK TOURISM PRODUCTS IN RWANDA

An inquiry was made to know the dark tourism products in Rwanda and in the table below, respondents indicated the examples and place that they believe could be classified as dark tourism product in Rwanda.

Note: Some of the products received multiple responses and thus presented as such

Table 1: Dark tourism products and place

Product	Location	No. of respondents	Percentage (%)
		Frequency	Percent
Ex. Rucunshu	Gitarama	41	95.3
Kigali memorial center	Gisozi	43	100.0
Musanze cave	Ruhengeri	39	90.6
Ntarama and Nyamata memorial site	Bugesera	40	93.6
Nyange high school	Ngororero	8	18.6
Habyarimana plane crash	Kanombe	40	93.6
Murambi memorial center	Nyamigabe	37	86.0
Bisesero, Gatwaro Stadium and Gitesi memorial site	Kibuye	35	81.4
Nyanza memorial site	Nyanza	22	51.1
Nyarubuye memorial site	Kirehe district	39	90.6
Church of Mubuga	Western province	33	76.7
Kibeho site	Nyaruguru	38	88.3
Butare stadium	Butare	41	95.3
Belgian memorial	Nyarugenge	12	27.9
Kabgayi church	Gitarama	43	100.0
National Heroes Memorial	Kigali	24	55.8
Total		**43**	**100.0**

Source: By the researcher 2012

From table I above, the results show the various dark tourism products in Rwanda. The findings noted that dark tourism products in Rwanda provide a bad on the reality of the past battlefields, disasters and the 1994 genocide in Rwanda. Owing to the lack of any records or data there is limited historical information on the growth and development of Rwanda's dark tourism products and that is why respondents were not able to identify the products but they do exist. Some respondents, however, suggest Rucunshu, Musanze cave, ex president Juvenile Habyarimana plane crash scene at Kanombe and various genocide memorials as the dark tourism products. The dark tourism products in the country are dignified and extremely well presented as the darkest chapter in Rwandan history, honoring the dead but also looking in the future. The products are chronicled with vivid images and horrifying video clips of the history of Rwanda in macabre details.

4.3 THE CHALLENGE OF PROMOTING DARK TOURISM IN RWANDA

Information was sought from respondents to know the challenges of promoting dark tourism in Rwanda

Table 2: Less effective information dissemination

	Strongly agree	Disagree	Agree	Strongly disagree	Total
Frequency No.	5	2	36	0	43
Percentages (%)	11.6	4.7	83.7	0.0	100.0

Source: By the researcher 2012

Information about whether less effective information dissemination system affected promotion of dark tourism was sought. From table 2, the results indicate that the majority of respondents 83.7% agree and 11.6% strongly agree well as 4.7% disagree. The findings indicated that less effective information dissemination systems has affected promotion of dark tourism in such a way that many tourists (domestic and international tourists) do not know the dark tourism attractions and destinations in Rwanda. This was partly attributable to the low efforts by tour operators in promoting dark tourism. As such, most tour operators have no marketing strategy for dark tourism to date because they do not consider this sector (dark tourism) important as they deal mainly with Nature or eco- tourism, a more lucrative sector.

Table 3: High cost charged to tourists

	Strongly agree	Disagree	Agree	Strongly disagree	Total
Frequency No.	0	4	0	39	**43**
Percentages (%)	0.0	9.3	0.0	90.7	**100.0**

Source: By the researcher 2012

Information was also sought to know whether High cost charged to tourists appear to affect the promotion of dark tourism. The results show the highest number of the respondents 90.7% strongly disagree and 9.3% disagree to the statement. The findings revealed that there is no fee charged on entry permits or tickets at various dark tourism sites.

Table 4: Insufficient dark tourist facilities

	Strongly agree	Disagree	Agree	Strongly disagree	Total
Frequency No.	24	0	19	0	**43**
Percentages (%)	55.8	0.0	44.2	0.0	**100.0**

Source: By the researcher 2012

About whether insufficient tourist facilities at key dark tourism sites affected promotion of dark tourism were inquired and from table 4 above, results indicate that 55.8% of the respondents strongly agree and 44.2% agree to the statement. The findings indicated that facilities are not sufficient at key dark tourism sites, including the Visitors centers, interpretation equipments, libraries, exhibitions and photos. Additionally, some attractions are located away from the city centers and accommodations facilities are inadequate or of poor quality and not available in some places.

Table 5: Negative perception and publicity

	Strongly agree	Disagree	Agree	Strongly disagree	Total
Frequency No.	28	0	15	0	43
Percentages (%)	65.1	0.0	34.9	0.0	100.0

Source: By the researcher 2012

An inquiry was made to know whether negative perception and publicity affected visitation to dark tourism sites and from table 5, the results indicates that, 65.1% of the respondents strongly agree and 43.9% agree. The findings revealed that Some of the foreigners only have knowledge of what happened 18 years ago in Rwanda and therefore think of Rwanda as an insecure, violent destination; a country in despair. This comes from the fact that most news media feature only the bad news from the region. On the other hand, failure to take cognizance of local citizens as stakeholder has depressed the spirit of local citizens to support dark tourism outreach activities.

Table 6: Lack of skilled staff

	Strongly agree	Disagree	Agree	Strongly disagree	Total
Frequency No.	11	2	30	0	43
Percentages (%)	25.6	4.7	69.7	0.0	100.0

Source: By the researcher 2012

Whether lack of skilled staff appears to affect the promotion of dark tourism in Rwanda was inquired and the results in table 6 indicate that the highest numbers of respondents 69.7% agree and 25.6% strongly agree well as 4.7% disagree. The findings indicate that lack of skilled manpower addresses the fact that there is a severe shortage of people with sufficient management and technical skills necessary to organize and sustain dark tourism in Rwanda.

Table 7: Infrastructures not being of the required level

	Strongly agree	Disagree	Agree	Strongly disagree	Total
Frequency No.	23	0	20	0	**43**
Percentages (%)	53.5	0	46.5	0.0	**100.0**

Source: By the researcher 2012

Information was also sought to know whether Infrastructures being not of the required level affected visitations to the dark tourism destinations in Rwanda. The results show that 53.5% of the respondents strongly agree and 46.5% agree. The findings indicated that most dark tourism sites still operates in abandoned buildings and even at some sites memorials like graves and tombs have not been erected. Additionally, the road network to most of the dark sites is of poor quality making the movement of tourists difficult.

Table 8: Other challenges

	Challenges		Total
	Limited finances	Poor quality of customer services	
Frequency No.	35	8	**43**
Percentages (%)	81.4	18.6	**100.0**

Source: By the researcher 2012

From table 8, results show other challenges to the promotion of dark tourism with 81.4% of the respondents indicating limited finances and 18.6% noted poor quality of customer services. The findings revealed that dark tourism sector lack funds for the construction and maintenance of sites, training of staff, purchase of equipments and other resources critical for development of the dark tourism industry. Additionally, Poor attitude, unpleasant behavior and poor services to tourists by some staff have in a way had a negative consequence on promotion of dark tourism.

4.4 MEASURES THAT COULD BE ADOPTED TO PROMOTE DARK TOURISM IN RWANDA

Table 9: Improve marketing strategies

	Strongly agree	Disagree	Agree	Strongly disagree	Total
Frequency No.	25	0	18	0	43
Percentages (%)	58.1	0.0	41.9	0.0	100.0

Source: By the researcher 2012

Whether Improve marketing strategies for dark tourism was inquired and the results in table 9 indicates that the highest number of respondents 58.1% strongly agree and 41.9% agree. The study noted that it is important for Rwanda Tourism Board to distributes literature to service providers regarding the importance and potential benefits of dark tourism, as well as successful advertising methods like website, audiovisual (films, video, CD), magazines, books, brochures and leaflets to attract more tourists to the dark tourism sites.

Table 10: Training of staff and service providers

	Strongly agree	Disagree	Agree	Strongly disagree	Total
Frequency No.	15	7	21	0	43
Percentages (%)	34.9	16.2	48.9	0.0	100.0

Source: By the researcher 2012

About Training of staff and service providers, results from table 10 above show that 48.9% of the respondents agree and 34.9% strongly agree well 16.2% disagree. The findings indicated that the training needs in tour guiding, customer care, management and marketing is away foreword to promoting dark tourism in Rwanda

Table 11: Networking and partnership with other stakeholders

	Strongly agree	Disagree	Agree	Strongly disagree	Total
Frequency No.	11	0	32	0	**43**
Percentages (%)	25.6	0.0	74.4	0.0	**100.0**

Source: By the researcher 2012

Information was also sought to know whether Networking and partnership programs with other stakeholders can boost dark tourism in Rwanda. The results show that the majority of the respondents 74.4% agree and 25.6% strongly agree. The findings noted that the purposes of these partnerships are to encourage joint ventures in order to build networks for information exchange. Addition to that, a key element of these partnerships is the development of a community based orientation programme that give local residents the responsibility of making sure visitors understand and appreciate the unique opportunity they have in visiting the dark tourism sites.

Table 12: Encouraging local population in Rwanda to visit dark tourism sites

	Strongly agree	Disagree	Agree	Strongly disagree	Total
Frequency No.	29	0	14	0	**43**
Percentages (%)	67.5	0	32.5	0.0	**100.0**

Source: By the researcher 2012

An inquiry was made to know whether encouraging local population in Rwanda to visit dark tourism sites has positive impact on promoting dark tourism and from table 12, the results indicates that, 67.5% of the respondents strongly agree and 32.5% agree to the statement. The findings noted that if the entire local population visits and understands the importance of dark tourism, there will then be millions of people out there doing dark tourism marketing for their country.

Table 13: Improve the variety and accessibility of dark tourism attractions

	Strongly agree	Disagree	Agree	Strongly disagree	Total
Frequency No.	21	0	22	0	43
Percentages (%)	48.9	0	51.1	0.0	100.0

Source: By the researcher 2012

Information about improving the variety and accessibility of dark tourism attractions, 51.1% of the respondents agree and 48.9% strongly agree. The findings indicated that, Rwanda Development Board should begin to identify and market underdeveloped and underutilized dark tourism attractions throughout Rwanda. Additionally, by reducing pricing and advertising low cost attractions throughout the country, tourists will be encouraged to travel to the dark tourism sites.

Table 14: Other measures

	Measures		Total
	valuation of employees	Financial support	
Frequency No.	12	31	43
Percentages (%)	25.6	74.4	100.0

Source: By the researcher 2012

From table 14, 74.4% of the respondents noted financial support well as 25.6% indicated valuing employees as some of the other measures to promote dark tourism in Rwanda. The findings revealed that, all management depends upon finance. Dark tourism management agencies must have sufficient funds to respond properly to the demands of dark tourism; funds may come from government, entrance fee per person or per vehicle or combination of both, donations and fundraisings. All dark site employees and volunteers need to be recognized as its valued ambassadors. They are, possibly, the most important single factor in ensuring the successful management of tourism in dark sites. Front-line workers especially, such as guides and staff in visitor centers, are the visible public expression of the management philosophy behind the dark site's operation. If the relationship between staff and visitors is positive, the benefits will be many.

CHAPTER FIVE

SUMMARY OF FINDINGS, CONCLUSION AND RECOMMENDATIONS

5.1 Summary of Findings

The results show the various dark tourism products in Rwanda like Ex. Rucunshu, Musanze cave, Kigali memorial center, Nyamata and Ntarama memorial sites among others that provide a grime check on the reality of the past histories in Rwanda. This was in relation to Keil, (2005) Dark Camps of Genocide, Keil noted that Dark Camps of Genocide represents those sites and places which have genocide, atrocity and catastrophe as the main product theme and thus occupy the darkest edges of the dark tourism spectrum and are produced to provide the ultimate emotional experience whereby visitors sightsee in the mansions of the dead. Dark Camps of Genocide tell the terrible tales of human suffering and infliction and consequently have a high degree of political ideology attached to them.

From the findings of the study, the highest number of respondents 58.1% strongly agree and 41.9% agree that Improving marketing strategies for dark tourism through distribution of literature to service providers regarding the importance and potential benefits of dark tourism, as well as successful advertising methods like website, audiovisual (films, video, CD), magazines, books, brochures and leaflets to attract more tourists to the dark tourism sites was one of the measures of promoting dark tourism in Rwanda. This was in accordance with Zelizer (1992) who noted that Modern media not only plays a role in disseminating information to the public off-site (thereby pushing visitors to the destination); it also plays an important role in the development of on-site interpretation (hence pulling visitors) and additionally, National Civil Rights Museum (2002) noted that numerous brochures of dark tourism sites offer artifacts in their marketing campaigns.

Results in indicated that, 83.7% of the respondents agree that less effective information dissemination system affected promotion of dark in such a way that many tourists (domestic and international tourists) do not know the dark tourism attractions and destinations in Rwanda. Addition to that, 66.7% of the respondents strongly agree that Infrastructures being not of the required level affected visitations to the dark tourism destinations in Rwanda. This was in relation to Poirier, (2000) that, lack of awareness and understanding by visitors of the excellent dark tourism destination in a country and the range of accommodation options and attractions available. Lack of resources and significant financial, cultural and infrastructural obstacles also hamper efforts aimed at promoting dark tourism, which would lead to a self sustaining industry.

According to the results of the study, highest numbers of respondents 50.0% agree and 33.3% strongly agree lack of skilled staff appears to affect the promotion of dark tourism in Rwanda. The findings indicate that lack of skilled manpower addresses the fact that there is a severe shortage of people with sufficient management and technical skills necessary to organize and sustain dark tourism in Rwanda. This was in line with Baum, (2007), he noted that, Notwithstanding the undoubted impact of technology on the distribution and delivery of dark tourism services, people remain a critical dimension within the successful delivery of dark tourism services. The story of successful dark tourism enterprises is one that is largely about people; how they are recruited, how they are managed, how they are trained and educated, how they are valued and rewarded, and how they are supported through a process of continuous learning and career development. In today's tourism environment, worldwide, the pressing issues facing the dark tourism sector relate to a combination of recruitment and retention; labor turnover; skills shortages; training and development opportunities; and workplace conditions.

5.2 Conclusions

As discussed in the findings, tourists are prevented from traveling to dark tourism sites due to several limitations such as lack of awareness, inaccessible transportation, inadequate facilities and poor quality of services. However, tourists must be motivated to participate in Rwandan dark tourism. Since the Rwandan dark tourism industry is still developing and is lacking in areas where other countries have succeeded, it is important to understand the successful practices in terms of management, development, branding, marketing, and pricing strategies.

Identifying the successful practices in management, branding, marketing, and pricing strategies of dark tourism attractions around the world can aid in applying these ideas towards improving the dark tourism industry in Rwanda. Several dark tourism sites in Rwanda have already become thriving attractions for dark tourism, but many have yet to be properly developed and branded and utilized. Combining these ideas with those from sites around the world can enable the application of these successful practices to new and already developing sites throughout Rwanda.

Thus, some of the products of dark tourism & measures have been adopted to promote dark tourism sites in Rwanda

5.3 Recommendations

When promoting Rwanda dark tourism, dark tourism site administrator should cooperate with each other in order to form special dark tourism routes. On the other hand, it should focus on its nearby attractions and properly optimize the usage of other resources. Dark tourism places also can cooperate with the local or international travel agencies, such as combining or adding the dark tourism sites to the organized tourism routes. Additionally, special theme tour concerning the day trip of dark tourism line or free guide route of dark tourism can be other suggestions.

Dark Tourism is a comprehensive social phenomenon which refers not only to route of travel options but also including the living conditions (hotels or hostels, food, transportation, shopping and entertainment of travel itself). Therefore, when exploiting the potential market of Rwanda dark tourism, the tourism operators should particularly consider other needs of tourists for the purpose of combining and optimizing all aspects of dark tourism resources. Ultimately, the aim is to make Rwanda dark tourism market outstanding among other nearby tourism sites.

Since we are living in a global world, using the mass media advertisements, specifically TV, Newspapers or other tourism information brochures is significantly important in attracting more dark tourists. Furthermore, efforts should be geared at expanding internet information or network in order to increase promotion trend. A large amount of travel agencies prepare lots of promotions and packages tour selling through internet.

Dark tourism programmes succeed when local peoples are involved. Therefore, local population living near dark tourism places must be involved in identifying, developing and planning for dark tourism in the area. Also, well trained tour guides who can interpret sites in a creative and exciting way are needed at all dark tourism places for a successful tourism experience.

Providing an enriching experience for visitors must be the goal of everyone in dark tourism. A common understanding of visitor needs and motivations by tourism operators and managers is the basis for providing high quality visitor experiences. High customer satisfaction is achieved through providing enjoyment for visitors, along with understanding of a place. Attention to detail and a commitment to high quality in the planning of activities, staff training, interpretation and provision of facilities and services will generate positive effects for promoting dark tourism places.

5.4 Further researcher

Finally the study recommends other researchers to carry out more research in the field of dark tourism in Rwanda. The argument in the next research study should be why dark tourism products in Rwanda are unutilized and under developed to the extent that most tour operators do not know of their existence.

REFERENCES

Blair, J. (2002). Tragedy turns to tourism at Ground Zero. The New York Times,

Bly, L. (2003). Disaster strikes, tourists follow. USA Today

Boorstin, D. (1964). The Image: A Guide to Pseudo-Events in America. New York: Harper and Row.

Body Worlds. (2008). Gunter von Hagens "Body Worlds". The Original Exhibition of Real Human Bodies

Buckart, A. J. and Medlik, S. (1974) Tourism, Past, Present and Future. London: Heinemann.

Daams, E. (2007). Dark Tourism: Bearing Witness or Crass Spectacle. Matador Net work.

Foley, M., and Lennon, J. (2005). Dark Tourism an old concept in a new world. TOURISM, The Tourism Society, Quarter

Foley, M., and Lennon, J. (1997). Dark Tourism. An Ethical Dilemma. In Strategic Issues for the Hospitality, Tourism and Leisure Industries, M. Foley, J.J. Lennon, and G. Maxwell. London: Cassell.

Foley, M. and Lennon, J. (1996). JKF and Dark Tourism: A Fascination with Assassination. International Journal of Heritage Studies

Galleries of Justice. (2005). Feel the Fear. www.galleriesofjustice.org.uk

Gilbert, M. (1986). The Holocaust: The Jewish Tragedy. London: Collins.
Keil, C. (2005) Sightseeing in the mansions of the dead. Social & Cultural Geography,

Kendle, A. (2006). Dark Tourism: A Fine Line between Curiosity and Exploitation. Vagabondish.

Lennon, J. and Foley, M. (2000). Dark Tourism: The Attraction of Death and Disaster. London: Continuum.

Lisle, D. (2004). Gazing at Ground Zero: tourism, voyeurism and spectacle. Journal for Cultural Research

MacCannell, D. (1989). The Tourist: A New Theory of the Leisure Class, 2nd Edition. New York: Schocken Books.

Mathieson, A. and Wall, G. (1982). Tourism: Economic, Physical and Social Impacts. London: Longman Cheshire.

Merrin, W. (1999). Crash, bang, wallop: What a picture, the death of Diana and the media. Mortality

Meyer, L. and Peters, J (2001). Tourism: A Conservation Tool for St.Louis Cemetery No 1. Dead Space Studio, University of Pennsylvania,

Northstar Gallery. (1998). Pere-Lachaise Cemetery: A Brief History

O'Neill, S. (2002b) Soham pleads with trippers to stay away. Daily Telegraph

Robinson, G. (2003). Tragedy's quiet side: Understated traveling exhibit leaves room for overpowering emotion. Oxford: Butterworth-Heinemann.

Rolfes, M. (2010). Slumming empirical results and observational theoretical considerations on the background of township, favelas and slum tourism. In R.Sharpley and P.R.Stone (eds) Tourist Experiences: Contemporary Perspectives, London: Routledge.

Rowe, M. (2007). Intrepid travelers break new ground. Daily Telegraph, 20th October,

Seaton, A. (1996) Guided by the dark: from thanatopsis to thanatourism. International Journal of Heritage Studies

Shackley, M. (2001). Managing Sacred Sites. London: Thomson.

Sharpley, R. and Stone, P.R. (2009) Life, Death and Dark Tourism: Future Research Directions. In R.Sharpley and P.R.Stone (eds) The Darker Side of Travel: The Theory and Practice of Dark Tourism, Aspect of Tourism Series, Bristol: Channel View Publications

Sharpley, R. (2005) Travels to edge of darkness: Towards a typology of dark tourism. In C. Ryan, S. Page and M.Aitken (eds.) Taking Tourism to the Limits: Issues, Concepts and Managerial Perspectives. Oxford: Elsevier,

Shaw, G. and Williams, A. (1994). Critical Issues in Tourism: A Geographical Perspective. Oxford: Blackwell.

Sindelaova, L. (2008). Terezin: The Darkest Places of Interest in the Czech Republic.

Smith, V. (1998). War and tourism: an American ethnography Annals of Tourism Research

Squires, N. (2004). New lease of life for war zone in paradise. Scotland

Stone P. R. and Sharpley, R. (2008). Consuming Dark Tourism: A Thanatological Perspective. Annals of Tourism Research,

Stone, P.R. (2005). Review: Niche Tourism: Contemporary Issues, Trends and Cases. Journal of Vacation Marketing,

Strange, C. and Kempa, M. (2003). Shades of dark tourism: Alcatraz and Robben Island. Annals of Tourism Research

Tarlow, P. (2005). Dark Tourism: The Appealing 'Dark' Side of Tourism and More. In M. Novelli, (ed). Niche Tourism: Contemporary Issues, Trends and Cases, Oxford: Elsevier.

Tercier, J. (2005). The Contemporary Deathbed: The Ultimate Rush. Basingstoke: Palgrave MacMillian.

Vega, C. (2002). Fast trade at ground zero. The Press Democrat

Verhela, P. (2011). Tourism School of Savonia University of Applied Sciences. Business Tourism and Management. TEAMS AND DEFINITIONS

Webber, S. (2007). 59 Dark Tourism. City Paper

Western Front Battlefield Tours. (2005). The Concept

Wight, C. (2006). Philosophical and methodological praxes in dark tourism: controversy, contention and the evolving paradigm. Journal of Vacation Marketing

Wight, C. and Lennon, J. (2004). Towards an Understanding of Visitor Perceptions of Dark' Attractions: The Case of the Imperial War Museum of the North, Manchester. Journal of Hospitality and Tourism,

Williams, P. (2004). Witnessing genocide: vigilance and remembrance at Tuol Sleng and Choeng Ek. Holocaust and Genocide Studies

APENDIX A: Letter addressing the intention of the research to respondents

The RTUC
P.0. BOX ...... Kigali
Tel:........................

17 October 2012

Dear Sir/Madam,

REQUEST FOR PERMISSION TO CONDUCT RESEARCH STUDY

I am **NIYOYITA Peace**; I am registered with the Rwanda Tourism University College for a bachelor's degree. The title of the intended thesis is *"challenges of promoting dark tourism in Rwanda"* I am expected to undertake research as part of the fulfillment of the requirements for the award of Bachelor of Travel and Tourism Management at RTUC

The purpose of this study is to find out the dark tourism products in Rwanda; investigate the challenges of promoting dark tourism in Rwanda and to establish measures that could be adopted to promote dark tourism in Rwanda.

I am writing to seek permission to go out to the field for the purpose of collecting information for the study

Please find attached copies of provisional questionnaire and interview guide for your perusal. Your favorable consideration will be much appreciated.

Yours sincerely

NIYOYITA Peace

APENDIX B : Questionnaire

QUESTIONNAIRE

Dear respondent,

You are kindly requested to respond to questions in the following questionnaire. The questions are related to challenges of promoting dark tourism in Rwanda. Your responses are of great importance as this survey forms an important part of a study.

Your answers will be treated confidentially and will only be used for the purpose of this research.

Thank you for your time.

Demographics Statistics of respondents

Please indicate the following with a cross on the appropriate response

1. Gender of respondent
   a) Male ☐
   b) Female ☐

2. category of respondent
   a) Tour operator ☐
   b) Museum manager ☐
   c) RDB staff ☐
   d) Memorial site ☐

3. How long have you worked in tourism industry?
   a) 1-5 ☐
   b) 6-10 ☐
   c) More than 10 year ☐

SECTION B:

Under this section, each question is presented as a statement. Please read the statement carefully before replying. You are asked to select one response that matches most closely with your perception of the statement.

THE DARK TOURISM PRODUCTS IN RWANDA

Definition

Dark Tourism is also called as black tourism or grief tourism which is not a very new activity or phenomenon in nowadays tourism market, it includes castles and battle fields, sites of natural or manmade disaster and the prisons that open to public.

Dark tourism is also defined as the act of travel and visitation to sites, attractions and exhibitions which have real or recreated death, suffering or the seemingly macabre as a main theme.
In the following table indicate the example and place that you believe can be classified as dark tourism product in Rwanda.

Two examples have been given in table for illustration:

Dark tourism product		Location/place
1	Ex. Rucunshu	Gitarama
2	Kigali memorial center	Gisozi
3		
4		
5		
6		
7		
8		
9		

THE CHALLENGE OF PROMOTING DARK TOURISM IN RWANDA

	STATEMENT				
	challenges of dark tourism	**Agree**	**Strongly Disagree**	**Disagree**	**Strongly Agree**
1	Less effective information dissemination system in promoting dark tourism				
2	High cost charged to tourists				
3	Insufficient tourists facilities at key dark tourism sites				
4	Negative perception and publicity about dark tourism sites				
5	Lack of skilled staff to effectively operate the tourists sites				
6	Infrastructures not being of the required level				

7. Any other challenges you think are hindering the promotion of dark tourism in Rwanda please put them in the space below

	STATEMENT	Agree	Strongly Disagree	Disagree	Strongly Agree
1	Improve marketing strategies for dark tourism				
2	Training of staff and service providers				
3	Networking and partnership with other stakeholders				
4	Encourage local population to visit dark tourism sites				
5	Improve the variety and accessibility of dark tourism attractions				

6. Any other measures you think can be adopted in the space below